THE GREAT BIG
WILD ANIMAL
BOOK

PICTURES BY
FEODOR ROJANKOVSKY

GOLDEN PRESS NEW YORK

Creak, creak, Father Bear bends down the branch.

The baby bears like to eat fresh, ripe berries.

Pad, pad, pad, goes Baby Elephant.

Tromp, tromp, comes Mother Elephant close behind.

Daddy Moose sniffs the clear woodland air.

He wants to be sure there is no danger near.

"Rooff!" says one little kit fox to his brother

while they pretend to fight over some strawberries.

"Humph!" says the haughty llama. "What are you doing

here on our high meadow in the mountains?"

Crunch, crunch, Mr. Beaver gnaws at a tender branch.

Slap, splash! Mr. Raccoon goes fishing with his paw.

"Hush!" says Baby Tiger Cub. "I hear something

in the grasses." Mother Tiger is listening too.

"Humph!" says the camel. "Walking over this lonely desert is enough to make anyone feel cross."

Mr. Rhinoceros and the frisky zebras are happy

to live near a pleasant jungle water hole.

"Stay away from my home!" roars lordly Father Lion.

He will not let anyone bother Mrs. Lion and their cub.

What a hot day! Hippo and Buffalo just stand

in the cool mud. But the flamingoes chatter and flap.

Mother Giraffe says "I love you" by licking her

baby's face, while the frisky antelopes frolic about.

"Stay there," says Mother Kangaroo to baby in her pouch

Mother and Baby Koala Bear are saying hello to you.

"Good morning," says the shy skunk, hopefully. But Mr.